ROLLS-ROYCE
HERITAGE

ROLLS-ROYCE HERITAGE

RICHARD BIRD

First published in Great Britain in 1995
by Osprey, an imprint of Reed Consumer
Books Limited, Michelin House,
81 Fulham Road, London SW3 6RB and
Auckland, Melbourne, Singapore and Toronto.

ISBN 1 85532 410 5

Project editor Shaun Barrington
Editor Julia North
Page design Paul Kime/Ward Peacock
Partnership

Produced by Mandarin Offset
Printed in Hong Kong

Front cover
*Terry Cohn's 1907 Roi des Belges
Rothschilds-bodied Silver Ghost
(see page 16)*

Back cover
*Tony Sobey's 1926 20hp; a superstar in
the UK during the early 1990s as
'Primrose' in the television series 'The
Darling Buds of May'*

Half title page
Ivan Odds' 1936 25/30 (see page 98)

Title page
*Mr Morley's 1946 Silver Wraith
(see page 112)*

Right
*Interior of 1921 Silver Ghost Brewster
Pickwick Sedan (see page 30)*

For a catalogue of all books published by Osprey Automotive
please write to:

**The Marketing Department, Reed Consumer Books,
1st Floor, Michelin House, 81 Fulham Road, London SW3 6RB**

Contents

P. Farnill's 1939 Wraith Park Ward Sports Saloon. Chassis no. WXA 89

Introduction

In a photographic essay such as this, there is no room for a full company history, but some introduction to the protagonists is surely required; and the fundamental reason why the cars of this most famous marque are such a satisfying subject for the photographer should be mentioned at the outset. Rolls-Royce was established in 1904 - incorporated in 1906 - by F. Henry Royce (born in 1863) and the Hon. Charles Stewart Rolls (born in 1877). It specialised in manufacturing a chassis and engine to customer requirements, after which a tailor-made body was built by a number of independent coach-builders designed to suit the customer's exact needs.

Royce and Rolls certainly came from very different backgrounds. Born at Alwarton in Northamptonshire, Royce was the youngest of five children, his father a mill manager. After the mill failed, Henry and his brother went with their father to London to find work. Despite his father's death at 41, the young Henry remained in London. He had a variety of jobs, from selling newspapers to delivering telegrams until, at the age of 14, an aunt obtained an apprenticeship for him at the Great Northern Railway Works at Peterborough, which was to become a stimulus for other British engineers, as well as the young Henry. Eventually, after three well spent years, his apprenticeship money of £20 per year ran out and Henry found a job working, for little reward, with a toolmaker in Leeds. By now the new world of electricity was beckoning, and he soon secured a job with the Electric Light and Power Co. in London. Eager to succeed by dint of hard work during the day and study at night at the London Polytechnic, Royce's diligence was acknowledged by his employers, who sent him to their Lancashire branch in Liverpool. The firm soon folded, and in 1884 the enterprising Henry took the plunge, deciding to start his own business – F. H. Royce & Co., with Ernest Claremont, a friend.

Concentrating on electrical equipment and working from rented accommodation in Cooke Street, Manchester, the £70 invested between them gradually grew into a profitable company, despite strong

W. Stansfield's 1936 20/25 HJ Mulliner Tourer. Chassis no GBK 39

competition from America and Germany. Even then, Henry Royce insisted on work of the highest quality, and this dedication to quality enabled a foundry and works to be established at Trafford Park, Manchester, which eventually went public in 1894. By 1899 the company's turnover was in excess of £20,000.

At this time there was a steadily growing motor industry in Europe and abroad but in part because of the strong anti-motor car lobby, there were few made in the UK. After an enforced holiday to South Africa, Royce bought a second hand French car, a 10hp two-cylinder Decauville on his return, and after his success with F. H. Royce Ltd, Henry was able to devote some time to car design.

Working in the retained old Cooke Street works, he used the French car as a base for a two-cylinder engine of nearly two litres. It had overhead inlet and side exhaust valves. As Royce always strived for perfection in all things he touched, only the highest quality materials were used. There was a live rear axle with a three-speed gearbox, and leather cone clutch. Braking worked via a handbrake on internal expanding drums and the footbrake operating on the propeller shaft. In all, three were made – one going to partner Ernest Claremont, and the third to Henry Edmunds, a motoring enthusiast and co-director in their electrical business. Edmunds was also a leading light of the Automobile Club of Great Britain, and a fellow member was Charles Stewart Rolls, the third son of Lord & Lady Llangattock.

Educated at Eton and Trinity College Cambridge, Rolls was a true aristocrat. He was perhaps unusual, though, in that he took an engineering course, and graduated with a keen interest in electricity. Rolls was also a keen motoring fan, having bought his first car, a French Peugeot, while still a student at Cambridge. He was later to experiment with De Dion, Leon Bollee and a racing Panhard. He also competed in most motoring formulas, and won the Automobile Club's 1000 mile Trial in 1900. In 1902 he formed C. S. Rolls & Co. to sell motor cars in Fulham, London, with show rooms in Brook Street, W1, and asked his friend and secretary of the Automobile Club, Claude Johnson, to join him. Knowing that Rolls was casting around for a British car to encourage British sales, Edmunds, who was very impressed with Royce's two-cylinder car, suggested Rolls meet Royce and test the car. A rendezvous was set for lunch at the Midland Hotel in Manchester, and the self-made man and the aristocrat met for the first time. Although they came from different backgrounds, there was much common ground between them: fundamentally a mutual appreciation of imaginative engineering, and perhaps also the bond of a keen interest in electricity. Rolls tried the Royce car, liked it, and the two agreed that Rolls would sell all the cars that Royce could make. It was named the Rolls-Royce.

C. Teissier's 1954 Silver Wraith Park Ward Drophead Coupé. Chassis no. BLW 77, registration no. 612 YYC

In 1904, *Autocar* printed the first Rolls-Royce advertisement, which described the car as "the first simple, silent Rolls-Royce", and in December of the same year, in Paris, the car made its international appearance with its now familiar hand-made 'Grecian' radiator. Royce had been experimenting, with Rolls' encouragement, with multi-cylinder engines while Charles Rolls, who was still very much involved with motor racing, entered the Tourist Trophy race on the Isle of Man with two of the now standard four-cylinder 20hp cars. The other driver was Northey. Rolls retired, due to gearbox trouble, but Northey finished second and, encouraged, Rolls decided to enter for the 1906 TT.

The 20 hp cars prepared were specially lightened, and dubbed the 'Light Twenty'. With Eric Platford (one of Royce's employees who had worked as an apprentice on the first two-cylinder car) as his mechanic/passenger, Rolls easily won with an average speed of 39.3 mph (63.3kmh). These racing exploits gave the new company valuable publicity, and Claude Johnson made the most of it. In 1906, C. S. Rolls and Co. and Royce Ltd. joined forces to become Rolls-Royce Ltd. Henry Royce's electrical firm F. H. Royce Ltd., was not part of this merger and

stayed independent. Claude Goodman Johnson's great ability as a public relations man became more apparent and he persuaded Rolls to drive a 'Light Twenty' from Monte Carlo to London in 37 hours and thirty minutes. One of the first publicity stunts.

Following Rolls' 1906 Tourist Trophy win, he also won a race at Yonkers and came second at Ormond Beach, America, against much larger engined cars. Claude Johnson himself drove the new 30hp six-cylinder car in the Scottish Reliability Trials and performed well, while the advertising slogan "The best in the World" was coined by Claude Johnson to advertise this model. This six-cylinder car, however, suffered from the same problem of severe crankshaft vibration that also plagued other manufacturers in the early days. Royce's answer to this was the introduction, six months later, of the six-cylinder 40/50. This car immediately put Rolls in front of the automotive pack when it made its

T.H.J Eastwood's 1929 20/25 Hooper bodied Coupé. Chassis no. GDP3, registration no. WM 5004

debut on the C. S. Rolls stand at the Olympia Motor Show in 1906. Two cars were exhibited, one with heavy limousine coachwork, to prove that the new chassis was capable of supporting the extra weight, and the other a tourer on a polished chassis.

Once again, Claude Johnson took advantage of the impact these cars were making on the motoring world, and silver painted and plated the polished chassis show car naming it 'The Silver Ghost'. Although the only wholly silver car, all the other Ghosts were called Silver Ghosts too. The meticulous attention to engineering detail by Royce, the drive and dash of Rolls, and the selling techniques of Johnson conspired to make the company a resounding success, and there was a need to find larger premises than the little Cooke Street works – Royce eventually settling on a new factory in Nightingale Road, Derby in 1907. The alliance was to end tragically in 1910, when Rolls was killed in a flying accident, with the terrible distinction of being the first Englishman so to die. It happened in a competition at Southborough near Bournemouth, after Rolls had acquired the flying bug from the Wright brothers at Kittyhawk when on a selling trip to the U.S.A. He had already become the first man to fly to France and back, non-stop. Royce, meanwhile, had been working flat out to satisfy the burgeoning order books, and suffering from exhaustion as well as the from the distressing news of his friend and partner's death, he decided to follow 'doctor's orders' and settled in the warmer, uncongested climes of Le Canadel, west of St. Tropez in the south of France, which had been introduced to him by Claude Johnson.

Here, in a house built to his own specification, he carried on with his design work during the English winters. But then came a relapse, and major abdominal surgery in England, followed by convalescence in Crowborough East Sussex. Eventually a house was found at West Wittering in Sussex from where Royce worked in the English summer, and then moved back to France at the onset of winter. This must have placed quite a strain on the works in Derby, who had to make Royce's designs work from such a long distance. By now, the design ethos espoused by Royce at the very beginning - of improving and polishing existing concepts rather than starting from scratch - was being followed by his team at Derby, and would continue long after his death in 1933, shortly after he had been made a Baronet.

The Silver Ghost 40/50 1906-1925

As previously mentioned, the Ghost made its first appearance at the Olympia Motor Show of 1906, causing a sensation. It was conventional in design, but had far more refinement than previous models. It had a six-cylinder side valve engine, the cylinders being in two blocks of three. The bore and stroke was 115mm x 115mm producing 7,036cc, and the crankshaft vibrations of the six-cylinder 30hp engine were subdued with a seven-bearing crankshaft of immense weight and strength.

All this was driven by a leather-lined cone clutch with a four-speed gear box on which there was overdrive on top gear, first introduced on the Light 20. This led through to a rear axle which was a little fragile on these early Ghosts, and was to be strengthened during the chassis redesign of 1911-12. At the same time, the chassis was beefed-up, as well as the crankcase, and a crankshaft damper was fitted. Suspension at the front was by semi-elliptic springs and the rear suspension was platform with the rear springs being linked by a transverse spring centrally located from the chassis. Braking was largely by handbrake, working on the rear wheels only, through internally expanding shoes on the rear brake drums, plus a foot brake operating on the propeller shaft, utilising metal shoes. Four-wheel brakes were introduced in 1924, and many owners took advantage of this significant improvement and subsequently had them fitted. The excellent electrics used dual ignition, magneto and trembler coil, each working independently on two spark plugs per cylinder.

With their lower set radiators and more delicate looks, the pre-war Silver Ghosts appear to some prettier than the later post-war models. The original chassis price was about £980.00.

The famous AX 201, one of two cars which first appeared at the Olympia Motor Show in 1906, with a polished chassis and later painted silver by Claude Johnson, and named 'The Silver Ghost'. In May 1907, under the watchful eye of the RAC, he started from Bexhill and drove to Scotland and back via Glasgow, using only top gear. The journey lasted 12 days, covering 2000 miles (3,200km), and averaged 20.86 mpg. The car was then entered in the Scottish Reliability Trial – it won a Gold medal. Subsequently, Claude Johnson then chalked up a new long-distance record of 14,371 miles (23,127km) non-stop, apart from the occasional punctures

Terry Cohn's 1907 Silver Ghost. What a superb example of the very beautiful and immediately recognisable Roi des Belges bodywork. This handsome example is by Rothschilds. With a registration no. of SX 48, and chassis no. 60712, the original owner kept the car until 1962, and it has had three owners since then. When Terry became the fifth owner in 1988 it was still totally original and underwent its first restoration. Unusually, it still has the original AA and RAC badges fitted to the car when new, which I believe is quite rare. Mechanically everything is as it should be, with the original trembler coil in perfect working order. In 1911, the original acetylene lamps were converted to the new electric lighting. With its correct and original instruments and overall appearance, it must be arguably one of the most original Ghosts around

K. Wherry's 1911 Silver Ghost Torpedo Phaeton. Known as the Melbourne Ghost, this car has a chassis and engine no. of 1606; registration no. is RR 1911. The original owner was Sir Samuel Gibson from Melbourne, Australia, who ordered the car on 4 November 1910. Testing began after completion on 7 April 1911, and it was delivered on 17 June 1911. Sold by the original family in 1927, it had three subsequent owners, until no longer used, and was eventually acquired by the enthusiast the late George Green in 1960. The present owners bought it in 1989 from the Green estate, and it was restored by R. A. McDermott & Co., Melbourne

Above

A. M. Mackay's 1912 Silver Ghost Hamshaw Limousine. With a chassis no. of 2036 and registration no. X991, this car has very striking and colourful coachwork, and is a regular at the Rolls-Royce Enthusiast Concours and Rally meets

Right and opposite

Ronald Skerman's 1913 Silver Ghost. This is a Robinson bodied car in the beautiful Roi des Belges light touring style, and has a chassis no. 2582 and registration no. RS 169. Ronald calls it an upmarket mobile home (!), which he has owned for fifteen years, and is seen here driving it on one of its many trips to France, in the Dieppe rally. It was one of the first to have electric lighting. Previously the Ghosts used acetylene and oil. During the winter there are many jobs to do; here, Bruce Dowell is cleaning the wheel rims of Ronald's car (opposite above) and putting on a coat of preserver to stop corrosion

Edna Woolett's 1913 Silver Ghost Torpedo Tourer. This car has the London to Edinburgh chassis based on the car in which Claude Johnson did his famous London-Edinburgh-London run, with the car locked in top gear and under the watchful eye of the RAC; he averaged 24.32mpg (38.9kml). Later, at the recently opened Brooklands, he reached a speed of 78.26mph (125.92kmph). These lightweight cars had a definite sporty look, and Edna's is no exception. It has a chassis no. of 2500E and a registration no. of AP 2507. The original owners were the Colman family (who gave their name to the famous mustard). The car was loaned to the war effort in 1915 – and was used by Lord Kitchener in France as a staff car. It was restored in 1960, and retains the original instruments. A clutch prop was used to keep the clutch plates apart during storage, as they are prone to sticking

Terry Cohn's 1913 Silver Ghost Kellner Touring. This Ghost is another car built on the London to Edinburgh chassis as an 'Alpine Eagle' tourer and is a rare, totally original replica of the team cars which in 1913 did so well in the Alpine Trial. It has chassis no. 2534, and registration no. 1913 R, and it is not hard to imagine those intrepid racers peering carefully at altimeter and temperature gauge as they crossed those mountain passes

J. Milverton's 1914 Silver Ghost Tourer. At Althorp in 1993, many Ghosts gathered for the re-enactment of their Alpine triumphs of 1913. This car was one of many there to see them off. It has a chassis no. 6TB and registration no. RR 1914

M. Panter's 1921 Silver Ghost Barker Tourer. Castle Ashby in 1992: a magnificent building providing the perfect backdrop for the Rolls-Royce Enthusiasts Club Concours and Rally. This Silver Ghost had just won a first prize, and was taking its place before the customary winners parade around the grounds. It has chassis no. 168 AG, and registration no. PC 5553

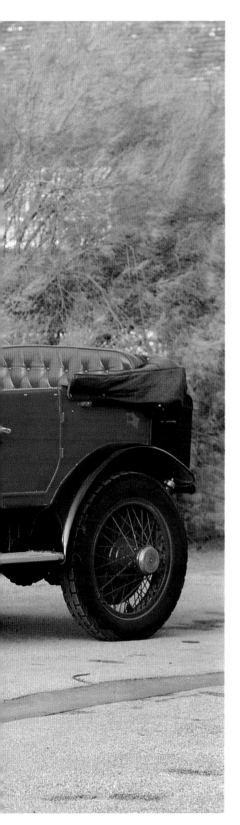

Brian Thompson's 1921 Silver Ghost Tourer. This car is unusual in that it has a Maythorn body that was originally fitted to a 1921 Sunbeam, and has been adapted to fit the Rolls-Royce chassis. It has chassis no. 18 NE, and registration no. XH 6538

These pages and overleaf

1921 Brewster Pickwick Sedan. After the war there were still many R-R people in the USA because of the production under licence of aero engines. As US import duty was high, Claude Johnson thought it a good idea to make cars there - for just the same reason that Honda build their GoldWings in America today!. Therefore a factory was established at Springfield, Massachusetts, and production began in 1921, continuing until 1931. Rather than follow the practice in England of building a chassis and engine only, and then fitting coachwork of the customer's choice, it was decided to follow American practice and supply the cars complete from the showroom. Brewster, a well known coachbuilders from New York, were chosen and many essentially American styles were built, although they were given very English names. This car has chassis no. 95 BG and registration no. DS 7421

Nick Channing's 1922 Silver Ghost Skiff. This car has a chassis no. 42 ZG and registration no. NN 3740. It was originally owned by Raleigh Bicycles chairman Hugh Bowden, and was a Barker Landaulette; it was re-bodied in the 1950s. It was one of many cars retro-fitted with the four wheel brakes (in 1925) when they became available in 1924. It is now used regularly by Nick

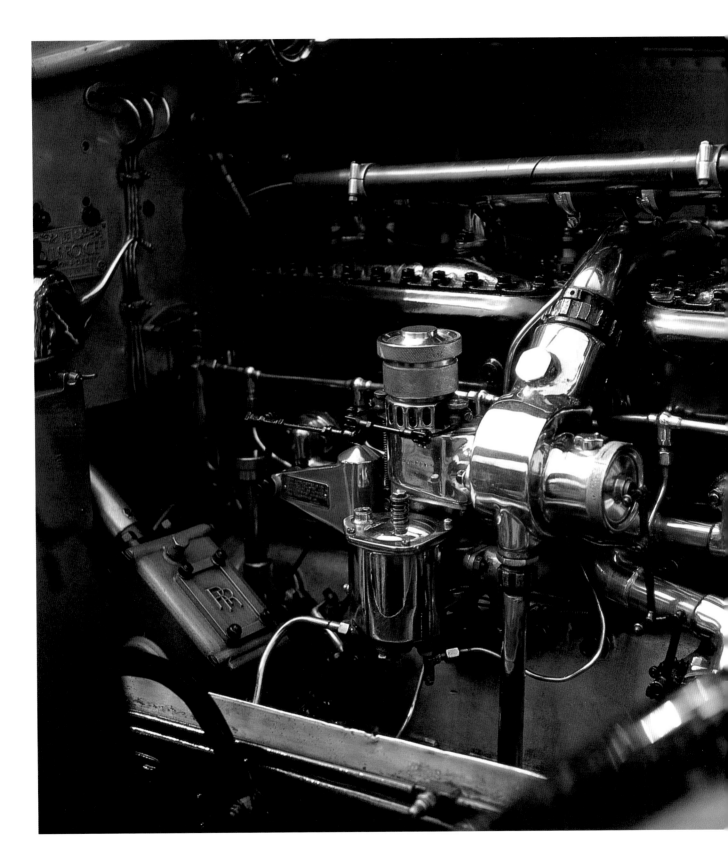

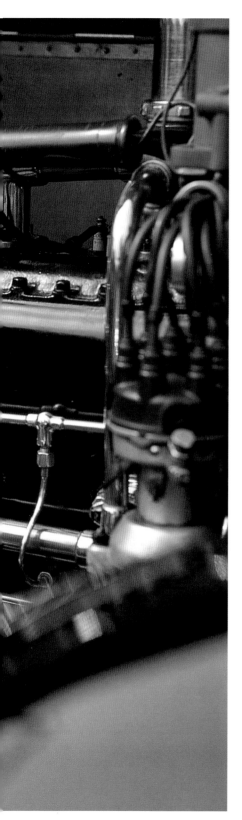

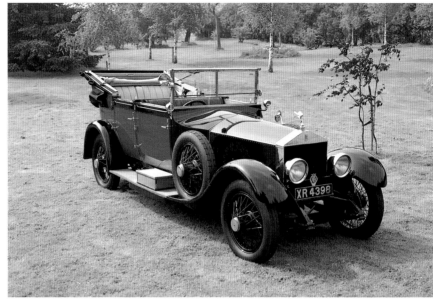

These pages and overleaf
Ivan Odds' 1923 Silver Ghost Hooper enclosed Cabriolet. This car was first owned by the Earl of Derby's family, and was sold with front wheel brakes, but they were not fitted until 1925 as they had not been 'perfected' by Rolls-Royce! Although built by Hoopers, the car is fitted with the rival Barker coachbuilders patented head lamp dipping system, whereby rods go from the head lamps to the driver's compartment, who operates a lever to dip them. In its early days, the radiator boasted a horse mascot in tribute to the Earl's 1924 Derby winner 'Sanso Vino'. It has chassis no. EM 36 and registration no. XR 4398

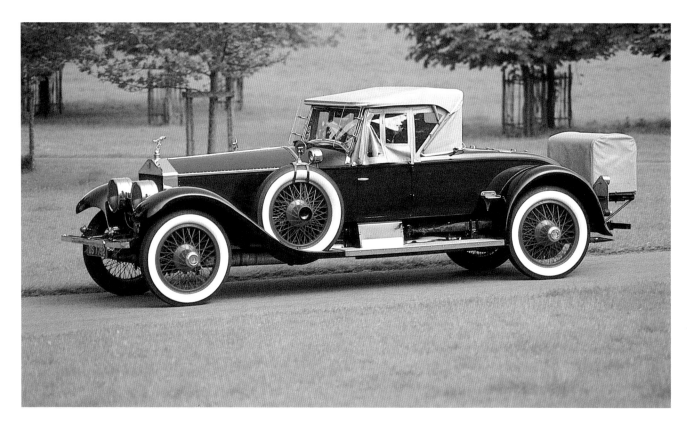

Above

T. R. Stone's 1923 Silver Ghost Piccadilly Roadster. Another fine example of the American Silver Ghosts made at Springfield, Massachusetts, with bright eye-catching red wire wheels and white-wall tyres. They were nevertheless pure Rolls-Royce under the bonnet. Chassis no. 401 HH, registration no. DS 7752

Above right

J. Jeeves' 1925 Silver Ghost Cassini Tourer. With chassis no. 62 EU and registration no. HNX 749T, this car is a good example of the later Silver Ghost, with its higher radiator and all-round imposing solidity

Right

B. Wootton's 1925 Silver Ghost Schaphandrier Torpedo. A most unusual wooden-bodied Ghost emulating the earlier light and sleek Torpedo bodies. Chassis no. 104 EU and registration no. E5 5540

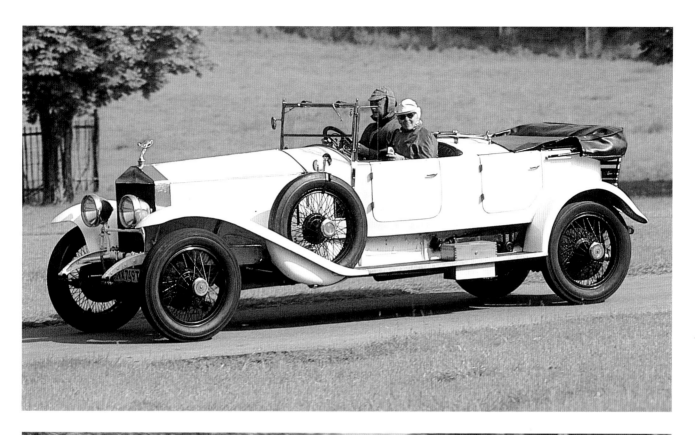

The Phantom I 40/50 1925-1929

By 1925, after a long run, the Silver Ghost had begun to look a little outdated, so a successor – the Phantom I – was introduced. It was built on the same chassis, but new life was breathed into it via a new engine. This still had six cylinders, but now had pushrod overhead valves with a larger 4 ½ x 5 ½ bore and stroke producing 7,668cc. Although beautifully constructed, it was rather untidy looking and possibly not quite as smooth as the Ghost engine. It had a single plate clutch and four-speed gearbox. Suspension was semi-elliptic at the front and cantilever at the rear. Four wheel brakes were now standard, incorporating the Hispano Suiza design of gearbox drive mechanical servo used by the Derby factory under licence giving, for 1925, state-of-the-art braking. There was an independent handbrake.

Perhaps the most important new development was the Rolls-Royce hydraulic shock absorbers introduced as a modification, and arguably the best around. This design remained with slight updating until, much later, gas filled telescopic dampers were used on the Silver Shadows. Another modification was the use of an aluminium cylinder head – it was good for heat transfer, but was to give restorers headaches in later years due to electrolytic corrosion of the water passages. Electrics were dual ignition, magneto and coil with a beautifully made distributor and governor underpinning the reliability of the product. The chassis price was approximately £1,850.

Right and overleaf
Ken Jenner's 1926 Phantom I Limousine de Ville. This very elegant Limousine de Ville by Hooper has a chassis no. of 53 DC and registration no. YP 9550. It was originally supplied to Mr. Hillier Holt, who lived at Rotherfield Place and London. He sold it in 1935 and it became the Mayoral car in York until 1959, when it was used by the High Sheriff. Notable passengers included George VI and HRH Queen Elizabeth

Above

C. Frost's 1926 Phantom I Tourer. A very handsome example of the new Phantom I enjoying the sun at Castle Ashby. Wheel trims instead of spokes make cleaning much easier and perhaps suit the style of the car better. By now the radiator had vertical shutters which were thermostatically controlled. The chassis no. is 46 LC and the registration no. YM 7193

Above right

G. K. Evans' 1927 Phantom I HJ Mulliner Sports Saloon. This powerful looking car is a product of the testing centre set up by Claude Johnson in 1924. It was bang in the middle of France at Chateauroux, where the long, empty roads provided the perfect place for a good thrash, and cars could be tested to destruction if needed. The chassis no. is 124 NC, registration no. YH 2819

Right

John Wilkes' 1928 Phantom I. This car was waiting for a little attention at Goudhurst Service Station where the Sargeants have been looking after Rolls-Royce and Bentley for many years. This one is a very fine replica-bodied example of the modern coachbuilder's art. Chassis no. 51 AL, registration no. YX 2592

The Phantom II 40/50 1929-1935

This car retained the Phantom I engine, although modifications were made to the inlet manifold which was moved to the offside, while a new, tidier design of exhaust manifold was on the nearside. In keeping with the Royce ethic of improving existing concepts, the cam went through several changes to help reduce sound levels at speed.

The main changes, though, were to the chassis and gearbox. The new chassis was lower, and incorporated semi-elliptic suspension all round, with ride control on the dampers. The gearbox was now integral with the engine, and was given synchromesh. With their new chassis allowing longer bonnet lengths and a higher waistline, these Phantom II's were some of the most graceful and stylish big cars ever made. They were also amongst the most reliable, due to their high quality electrics.

Incidently, these cars were amongst the first, in 1931, to be exported to America with black badges, after complaints from customers that the customary red badge clashed with many colour schemes, thereby belying the rumours that the black badge was an act of mourning for Royce, who died in 1933.

H. Prew-Smith's 1929 Phantom II Wilkinson Open Tourer. By now, some of the designs appearing from the various coachbuilders of the day were showing the classic big car lines, allowed to refine their techniques as the new chassis encouraged them to make the most of their skills. Chassis no. 66 WJ and registration no. UW 5531

Above

Philip Walker's 1930 Phantom II H. J. Mulliner. A gleaming example of the classic lines of the formal coachwork produced for the Phantom's chassis by H. J. Mulliner, a London firm established in 1900, from the older company of Mulliner of Northampton. They were eventually taken over by Rolls-Royce in 1959, and merged with Park Ward, who were also owned by Rolls-Royce, forming Mulliner Park Ward. It has chassis no. 190 GY and registration no. GK 64

Right

Ken Jenner's 1930 Phantom II Hooper Sedanca de Ville. This example demonstrates the low sporty looks these cars were now achieving. It started its life in Belgravia (and would have cut quite a dash) and then visited Canada in the '60s and '70s, making more friends. It is now happy in the depths of the Kentish countryside, with Ken at the wheel. Ken has owned her since 1988, and has given the car a mechanical overhaul. It has chassis no. 29 GY and registration no. GH 29570

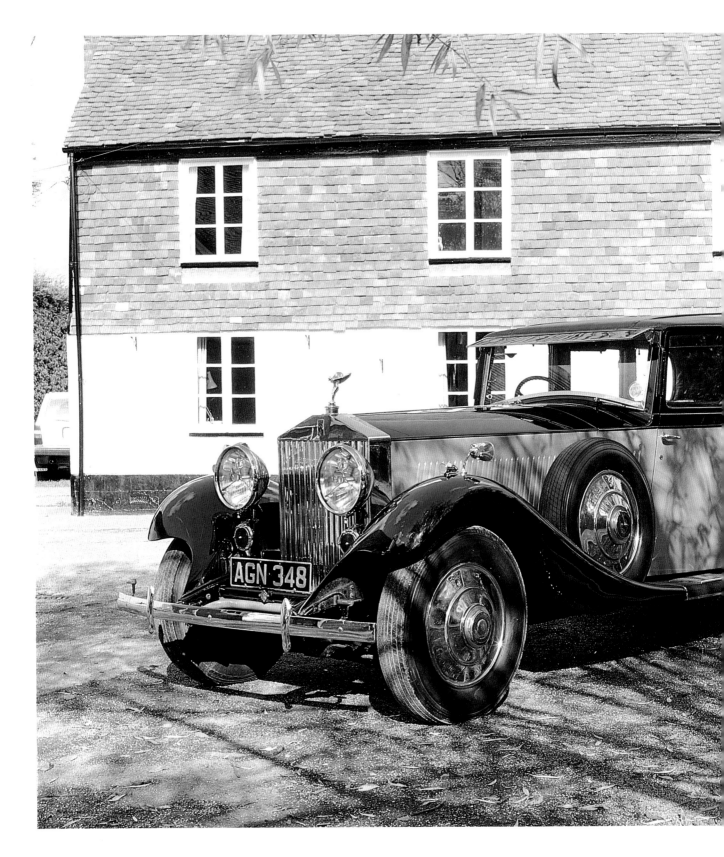

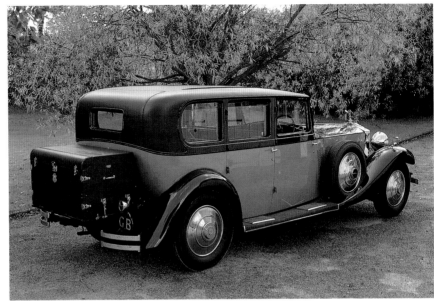

These pages and overleaf

Tony Sherwood's 1933 Phantom II Barker Saloon. Tony's car has an extra long wheelbase, which was ordered by its first owner Lord Percy Douglas Hamilton, Governor of Cape Province in South Africa, who wished to use the car for diplomatic duties. It eventually went to America, where Tony bought it and brought it back to England. It is completely original and is certainly a magnificent and statesmanlike machine. It has chassis no. 29 MW, engine no. F 645 and registration no. AGN 348

Above

P. Blond's 1933 Phantom II Continental. As the new lower chassis allowed more stylish coachwork, Royce, inspired by the looks of the Riley Nine/Sprite and wishing for a sportier line, designed a new sleek 'close-coupled' body for his own use, whereby the rear passengers' feet were under the front seats. This lightweight, sporting body became the precursor of the beautiful Continentals. This Phantom II Continental has a body by the Bromley firm of James Young, and carries two spare tyres, just in case. It has chassis no. 64 MY and registration no. AGH 1

Above right

Tom Mason's 1933 Phantom II Continental. The original owner was Allen Ansell, who ordered 'dual horns', the first car to be fitted with them. It also had the new type air silencer which had an extra 8in. of exhaust pipe at the back to clear the car. Another first was the employment of the new semi-expanding carburettor. It has a short wheelbase chassis, and included amongst the instruments is an altimeter for the mountain passes. It has chassis no. 72 MY and registration no. AGX 31, and embodies the classic looks of the Phantom Continental

Right

E. D. Evans' 1934 Phantom II Hooper Sedanca de Ville. What an eye catcher this is, with its bright colours and lovely flowing lines; the epitome of the large, luxury car. Chassis no. 11 RY and registration no. AXP 1

The Phantom III
1936-1939

With the introduction of the Phantom III, Rolls-Royce were again challenging other makes. These cars had even more speed than before, and the handling was very much improved. The Second World War would of course intervene in their production.

Royce had been experimenting from the early days with multi-cylinder engines, and using experience gained from his work on aero engines produced a V12 engine for the Phantom III. This had 12 cylinders with overhead valves, and a bore of 82.5mm and stroke of 114.3 producing 7,338cc. The valve gear functioned by use of pushrods and rockers via hydraulic tappets, which were eventually replaced by conventional solid type. The power from this well-balanced engine was delivered in a much smoother fashion, helped by the new stiffened chassis. This was accomplished by reverting to a separate gearbox placed well back from the engine. The ensuing space allowed a bolt-in cruciform to be added just behind the engine, giving much greater rigidity. All this new power was well matched with a new enclosed coil spring and wishbone independent front suspension developed from America. The rear suspension was still semi-elliptic. With its more rigid chassis frame and softer springing, the ride and handling made it a joy to drive. Chassis price was about £1,850.

J. Durham's 1936 Phantom III HJ Mulliner Sports Saloon. Most of these big Phantoms were very impressive, and this example is no exception. In the gradual switch to other manufacturers, a dual choke downdraught carburettor, not Rolls-Royce, but Stromberg, was specified on the V12. It has chassis no. 3 AX 143 and registration no. DUV 166

Above

P. J. Matthews' 1938 Phantom III Wilkinson Tourer. Another interesting body that demonstrates the independent coachbuilders' art, ensuring that no two Rolls-Royces were the same. This one has further seats behind, rather in the manner of the old Doctor's Coupe of the 20hp. It has chassis no. 3 DL 6 and registration no. FSU 122

Left

S. Barraclough's 1939 Phantom III Hooper Sedanca Coupe. Apart from the excellent Lagonda V12, designed by W. O. Bentley and Stuart Tresilian, Rolls-Royce had a virtual monopoly on the European luxury car market, with perhaps only Hispano Suiza left to challenge them. They too, however, were soon to go under. This 1939 P. III from the Isle of Man, has an appropriate registration number, and carries both the Blue rosette for Elegance and the Yellow rosette for second place, in the 1992 Concours at Castle Ashby. It has chassis no. 3 DL 62, and registration no. of P III MAN

ROLLS-ROYCE PORTFOLIO

In a book of this kind we cannot, of course, include every example of the coachbuilder's art that has graced the Rolls-Royce marque in the early years. In an attempt, therefore, to indicate the riches untapped, here is a selection of some of the many wonderful cars that attended the Rolls-Royce Enthusiasts Concours and Rally at Althorp Park in 1994.

1922 Silver Ghost Barker Cabriolet de Ville

1936 25/30 Windovers Roadster

1934 20/25 Barker Sports Saloon

1934 20/25 Windovers Landaulette de Ville

1937 25/30 Thrupp & Maberly Sports Saloon

1933 20/25 Lamorna Drophead Coupé

A later, Silver Cloud visitor

1937 Phantom III Hooper Sports Limousine

20hp Tourer (unidentified)

1930 20/25 Hooper Enclosed Limousine

1934 20/25 Gurney Nutting Sports Saloon

1932 20/25 Thrupp & Maberly Limousine

25/30 Limousine (unidentified)

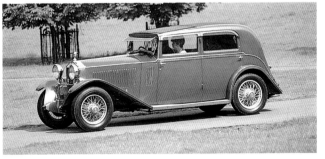

1931 20/25 Barker Sports Saloon

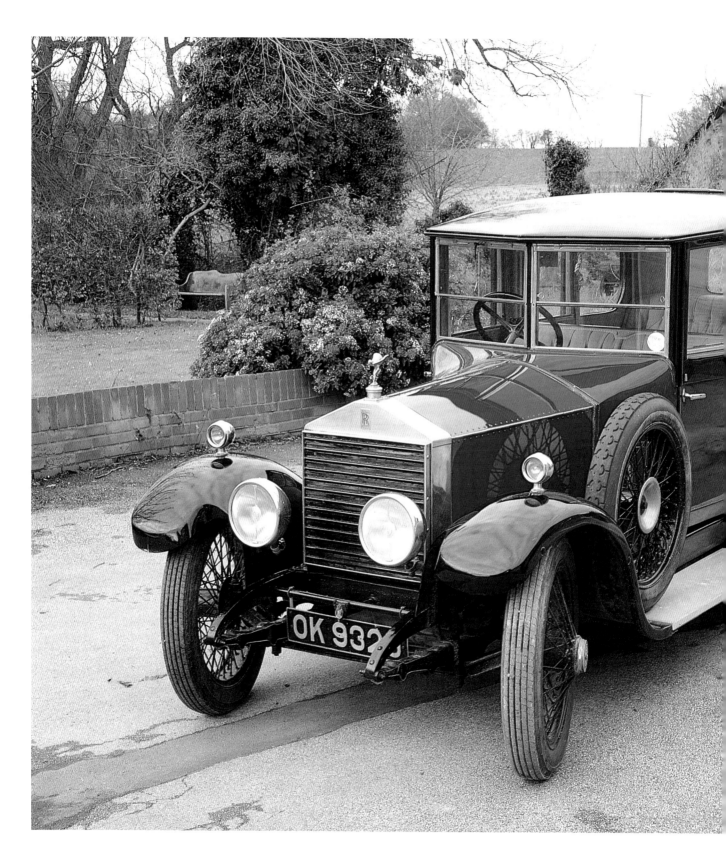

20hp Cars 1922-1929

From the beginning, the master plan was to make both a large engined car (40/50) and a small engined car (20hp) together. The 20hp also had a six cylinder engine, but differed from the Ghost in that it had overhead valves, with a bore of 76mm and stroke of 115mm producing 3150cc. Power output was smooth, and helped by an extremely heavy flywheel, but was intentionally limited, affecting the performance. There was a single plate clutch with a three-speed gearbox, operated via centre change, and braking was by independent foot and hand brake, both working on the rear wheels. During 1925, following the principle of improving the original, a four-speed gear box and right hand change was implemented, and this update was also joined by four-wheel brakes utilising the familiar gearbox driven mechanical servo. Suspension was half elliptic front and rear. Chassis price was about £1,100.

Brian Thompson's 1923 20hp. This original bodied car has coachwork by Flewitt, but probably is not in the original colours. It has a centre change gearbox which was only incorporated for about a year. It also has a curved radius radiator, of which Royce disapproved. They were also replaced after about a year with the favoured razor edged design of radiator

Ivan Odds' 1923 20 hp. This most original Hooper bodied Open Drive Landaulette, still has its 1923 leather hood and seats, and must be one of the earliest cars to be fitted with electric communication - a dictograph between passengers and driver. It can easily be identified as an early car, as it has the rare, round edge radiator and black painted tin plate shutters. Only a few of the early cars were fitted with this radiator. It has chassis no. 77 A 6 and registration no. PD 7611

Bob Hollamby's 1924 20hp. A nice example of a Barker bodied barrel-sided Tourer. Barker were a very old London coachmakers, established in 1710. They eventually went into liquidation in 1938, along with many other firms around that time, and were taken over by Hoopers. Bob's car has the Ostlers rear window fitted as standard, and the distinctive hand operated horizontal radiator shutters of the 20hp. It has chassis no. GRK 46 and registration no. NT 5278

Ivan Odds' 1925 20hp. This Brougham Coupe has a coachbuilt body by Lawton-Goodman. It was first owned by J. B. Joel, a well known South African diamond millionaire, and uncle to the famous Woolf Barnato of Bentley racing repute. He had the coachbuilders copy the design of his 1914 Renault Brougham. Robert Lawton-Goodman of the coachbuilding firm remembers the car when he was a schoolboy. Apparently Mr Joel bought the car for his wife, but also promised it to another lady of his acquaintance, and they both went to view the car on the same day! He remembers it as being a most embarrassing incident, calling, no doubt, for a great deal of tact and diplomacy. It has chassis no. GK 59 and registration no. RO 1883

Ken Jenner's 1925 20hp. Ken's car has a very pretty body by the French coachbuilder, Gallé of Boulogne-sur-Seine, Paris. It was the only one built by that company to be mounted on a 20hp chassis. Gallé did, however, build two Phantom I bodies for the King of Morocco. Previously, the car spent many years in Quebec, Canada, owned by the late Gaetan Trottier, until 1989, when Ken acquired her. It was the 17th car of the first series fitted with four wheel braking, and has a chassis no. GPK 17, and registration no. RR 5625

1926 20hp Shooting Brake. This car was waiting for a new owner at David Baldock's garage in Goudhurst. Quite rare, these shooting brakes would definitely have enough room for a pheasant or two, the Purdeys and the muddy boots. It has chassis no. GSK 1 and registration no. PE 8059

Another very attractive 1926 20hp, this time with a Doctor's Coupé body by William Arnold of Manchester. It has chassis no. ACK 79, and registration no. DN 8333

Above

K. Jay's 1927 20hp. Another Doctor's Coupé basking in the sun at the yearly Rolls-Royce Enthusiasts meet. This is the 1992 event, at Castle Ashby. The following year they were to meet at Althorp Park, home to the Spencer family. Always a great sight, about 2,000 of these most British of cars all together. It has chassis no. GHJ 40 and registration no. YH 793

Above right

Karl Foulkes-Halbard's 1928 20hp. The original owner of this Weymann fabric-bodied Saloon was Sir Malcolm Campbell. It was delivered to him on 20 August 1928 at 7 St. James St. SW1, order no. R 3589, at a discount of 12%. It was supplied with a nickel finish radiator, and raked steering column. It has chassis no. GBM 63 and registration no. XV 1227

Right

Tony Sherwood's 1929 20hp. This Sedanca de Ville has coachwork by the well established company of Thrupp & Maberly. It had been off the road since 1960, when Tony bought it from a concert pianist who had been planning to restore it, but never in fact got round to it. Tony then restored it himself, and found it a very satisfying car to drive. He has recently sold it

20/25 Cars 1929-1936

Towards the end of its production, the lack of power on the 20hp, added to the increasing weight of the formal coachwork being used, resulted in the bore increase and birth of the 20/25. The new bore was 82.6mm and stroke of 114.3mm producing 3,680cc. Compared to the 20hp it was rapid, but still suffered from the old Rolls-Royce problem of kick-back through the steering wheel when travelling at speed. However, the general handling and ride was good. It had the single plate clutch with four-speed gearbox, and eventually synchromesh as well. Braking was now four wheel with a servo, and an independent handbrake. Suspension was a semi-elliptic front and rear, and there was centralised chassis lubrication. Continued improvement being the policy, the 20/25 was later fitted with a Borg and Beck clutch, indicating the problems R-R were having in the costs of manufacturing their own components. Chassis price was about £1,185.

Left
Michael Tyler's 1930 20/25. This H. J. Mulliner fabric-covered Saloon is undergoing restoration at Sargeant's of Goudhurst. The trim work is being undertaken by its owner

Right
Mrs Tom Mason's 1930 Hooper bodied 20/25. This car has been restored where necessary to its original specification, and has the Hooper Patent quick action Signal Window. This works by pressing down the window with the hand to open, then the window is released by pressing a knob which is handily placed for operation by the elbow. It has chassis no. GGP 36 and registration no. GF 4756

Tom Mason's 1931 20/25. Bought by Tom many years ago in a completely dismantled state (the infamous 'box of bits'), this Windovers Sedanca de Ville has only just been restored to a finished state. Inside fitments are all silver plated, and there is a cocktail cabinet in the back in which is incorporated an altimeter, speedo, clock and temperature gauge. Looking at it, the wait was well worth it. It has chassis no. GNS 75, and registration no. GK 5070

Above
Mrs Norah Morley's 1932 20/25. Known in the family as
Emma, this two door fixed head coupe with coachwork by
William Arnold of Manchester was unfortunately languishing in
the garage with an oil leak. It has chassis no. GFT 68 and
registration no. XJ 811

Above right
A. Archer's 1933 20/25. An extremely elegant Gurney Nutting
Drophead Coupe, which, to back up my words, had just won the
Blue rosette for Elegance at the Concours and rally meet at
Castle Ashby, and was taking bows on its triumphal run round
the grounds. It has chassis no. GYD 26, and a registration no. of
BLO 442

Right
D. C. A. Bird's 1933 20/25. A very pretty example of an H. J.
Mulliner Sports Saloon, flying along at Althorp. For some people
the 20/25 series was the most attractive. This car has chassis
no. GTZ 66, and registration no. LS 6151

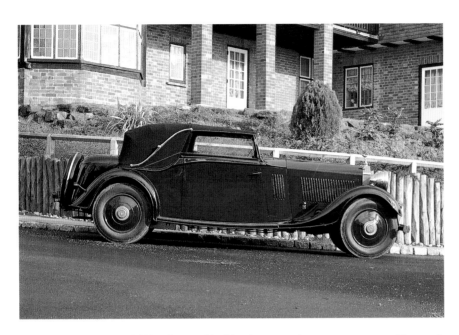

David Baldock's 1934 20/25 Convertible. Here's a nice elegant sports car, a Thrupp & Maberly convertible; just the job for a spin in country lanes, no matter that they're a bit muddy. This one has a covered spare tyre with the entry to the boot above it. On some models the spare lies on the opening, making it very heavy to open, bearing in mind that they were not sprung and just fell open. It has chassis no. GNC 67 and registration no. LSK 129

S. P. Simpson's 1934 20/25. This rear view of a Windovers Landaulette de Ville shows off the distinctive D-shape on this body style. It has chassis no. GED 37 and registration no. BGP 195

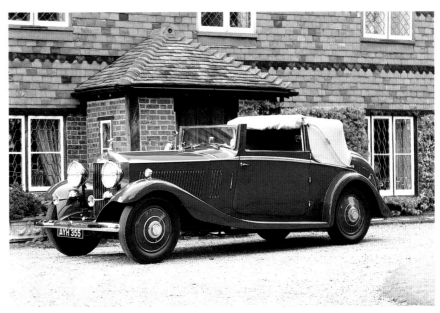

Bob Hollamby's 1934 20/25. Built by the coachworks of John Charles in the Great West Road, this car is the only one made by them in this style on a 20/25 chassis. (They only made three bodies in all for the 20/25, before one of the partners died and they ceased production.) The original owner was Captain Coburn, an MP for a North London constituency. The car was exported to Houston in 1964, and restored in America, where it was a National Concours winner. Bob bought the car in Houston in 1989. It has chassis no. GUB 59 and registration no. AYH 355

Dave Willoughby's 1934 20/25. This Thrupp and Maberly Limousine has the division for a chauffeur and unusually there is a sliding sunshine roof provided for him, normally associated with the owner/driver cars without the division. Originally black, the car has been restored by Dave and re-painted in ivory and black, considerably lightening her appearance. It has chassis no. GYD 8 and registration no. BGU 860

Bob Hollamby's 1935 20/25. This Hooper bodied Saloon originally belonged to Lady
Gowrie, and it remained in the same family from new until 1970. Bob bought her from
the second owner who lived in Marlborough, becoming only the third owner. The car
has been meticulously looked after and, unbelievably, both the interior and the red
paint on the outside are original and untouched – the black paint on the outside being
the only thing to be restored. It has chassis no. GBK 17 and registration no. CLL 938

Brian Thompson's 1936 20/25. This 20/25 has a body by the coachbuilders Martin Walters, who had coachworks at Folkestone in Kent. It was named a Wingham Cabriolet after a village nearby. It has chassis no. GBK 5 and registration no. CLL 185

25/30 Cars 1936-1938

The next logical step from the 20/25 was again to bore out the engine to its maximum potential of 89mm and stroke of 114mm producing 4,257cc. The chassis was the same as the 20/25, but by now the trend of using other manufacturers' products was becoming normal practice, and again a Borg and Beck clutch was used and a multi-jet downdraught Stromberg carburettor with SU petrol pumps. Steering was Marles cam and roller. The 25/30 with the lighter body styles was a fairly fast and silent car and speeds up to 80mph were possible. Other extras were the DWS permanent jack system and, again, a centralised lubrication system, activated by a pedal.

Ivan Odds' 1936 25/30. Another of Ivan's cars in his house livery of red and black. There is no doubt that these colours definitely suit the style of the Rolls-Royce. This one is coachbuilt by Windovers as a Landaulette, and its claim to fame is having Winston Churchill as a passenger when he toured Glasgow in the 1950s. It has chassis no. GAN 55 and registration no. WFX 465

Gerald Wallace's 1936 25/30. This style of colour scheme certainly works well, with the body shape on these saloons retaining the formal looks, but also slimming them down. At the time of writing, Gerald has owned the car for thirteen years, and says his Mann Edgerton coachbuilt car does about 8mpg around town. Tyres, however, are the highest running cost on the heavier bodied cars. It has chassis no. GGM 12 and registration no. PCE 626

The Gidwaney 1937 25/30. A splendid and unusual body shape – the rear spats adding to the sleekness of this Gurney Nutting coachwork

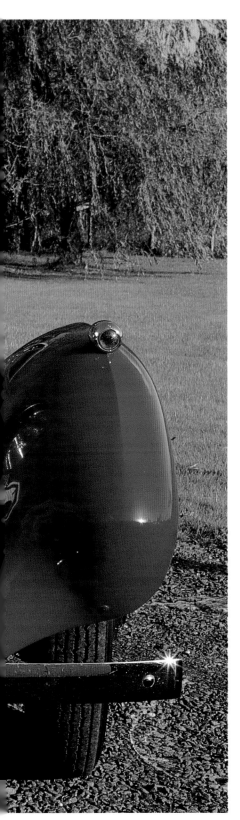

Owned by the Gidwaney family in India, this 25/30 is one of only two made with this body style, and when photographed was in England for restoration by Sargeant's of Goudhurst. It has chassis no. GRO 48 and registration no. BRG 1

E. Barrass' 1937 25/30. This handsome Barker Sports Saloon has an interesting war history: it was used by VIPs of the RAF (Air Commanders only), and would have been khaki. It has been returned to its original striking colour of French blue, and also retains its original upholstery. Eric still uses the car regularly as his main form of transport, with over 280,000 miles on the clock. When this photograph was taken, he had just done 1085 miles over the last seven days. It has chassis no. GHO 18 and registration no. CTC 77

A. J. Williamson's 1938 25/30. Distinctive pram irons on this Freestone and Webb fixed head Coupe. The extra power squeezed from the 20/25 engine provided 8–10 mph more than the maximum speed for the 25/30. There was also more low speed torque and acceleration

25/30 Wraith 1938-1939

The Wraith was the last small engined pre-war car to be built at Derby, before production resumed after the war at Crewe. It was, in reality, very similar to the Phantom III, with the P. III's layout and suspension. The engine was the same bore and stroke as the 25/30 but transformed to such an extent that substitution of parts was not possible. Its updated and stiffer chassis along with the modern softer springing allowed a very smooth and silent ride. This was of great help to the traditional coachbuilder who was used to dealing with the intractability of most vintage chassis. Chassis price was about £1,100.

Above

M. Bason's 1939 Wraith. This Park Ward Limousine has a division for the chauffeur. After the war more cars were made without the division, catering more for the owner/driver. It has chassis no. WRB 64 and registration no. FLU 672

Left

S. Carter's 1939 25/30 Wraith. A nice colour scheme on this fairly rare H. J. Mulliner Razor-Edge Saloon. Not many of these cars were made, because of the impending war. The white wall tyres finish the whole effect off nicely. It has chassis no. WKC 4 and registration no. LMC 705

Post World War II
Silver Wraith 1946-1958

After the war, manufacturing costs were closely reviewed and, in order to lower costs and hasten production, a new simplified chassis and engine were designed. Due to the escalating costs, the Rolls-Royce principle of providing chassis and engine only and the customer then having a body made by an independent coachbuilder was coming to an end. However, there was still public demand for this method, and the new simplified chassis and engine were requested by customers so that they could use their own coachbuilder as before. This produced the Silver Wraith, to some the last 'real' Rolls-Royce.

The new strengthened chassis had a suspension based on the pre-war cars, with independent front suspension in co-operation with unequal length wishbones and coil springs. Roadholding and comfort was very much improved, and was judged to be superior to that of American counterparts. The updating of the suspension went a long way to improving the wear on the components, and thus the life of the system. The kingpins had roller bearings, and the upper-outer wishbone pivot had a rubber bonded Silentbloc bush. The lower wishbone was fixed by means of a very stiff radius arm, attached at the back by a large ball which, in turn, was fixed to a socket below the chassis frame. The top wishbone was in conjunction with the well known R-R piston-type hydraulic shock absorber, which was still highly rated, one of the components still manufactured by R-R! Fixed into this latest chassis was a new six-cylinder power plant. Constructed as a straight six in a single

Mr Morley's 1946 Silver Wraith. This Hooper bodied Limousine with a split side bonnet is number 20 out of a model run of only 22. With its original colours of Caribbean blue and black it looks stunning, seen here near the sea at Cliftonville. It also retains the early original painted wheel trims, and Hooper door handles. There are no chromium mouldings on this model. The original owner was Sir John Jarvis, and it stayed in the family until sold to Denys Eyre Bower of Chiddingstone Castle. The present owner is the third owner in forty-eight years. It has chassis no. WTA 20 and registration no. LPB 1

unit cylinder block and crankcase of cast iron, it had a bore of 88.9mm and stroke of 114.3mm producing 4,257cc, and reverted to an overhead inlet and side exhaust valves, similar to Royce's design on his first two-cylinder car of the early 1900s. Its seven main bearing, entirely machined, crankshaft and bolt-on balance weights gave a very refined ride. With the new engine came a four-speed gearbox – much praised for its smooth and exact gearchanging which R-R were hard pressed to improve. The braking system was Lockheed hydraulic at the front with adjustment using a Girling type expanding-shoe pivot. Rear brakes were Girling expanding wedge with the usual R-R mechanical servo. Chassis price was about £1,800.

Ivan Odds' 1947 Silver Wraith. This Silver Wraith Sedanca de Ville, with coachwork by H. J. Mulliner, was the first Rolls-Royce shipped to Hong Kong after the war. It remained in the same ownership until purchased by Ivan in 1988. The car has covered less than 50,000 miles from new. It has chassis no. WYA 32 and reg. no. LSU 833

Terence Morley's 1949 Silver Wraith. Only seven cars with this style of Hooper coachwork were made. Of these seven, six were owner/driver, like this one, and one had the division for a chauffeur. Terence's car is unique in that it is the only one with the big P100 headlamps. With a design no. of 8181, it is a sister car to the one made for the Maharaja of Mysore, and looks similar from a distance, but is very different inside. Hooper were known for being quite inventive in their bodies, and were always looking for the new and unusual. This style of body pre-empted the later Empress line, with its curved windscreen and dashboard, while also incorporating the earlier spats (covered wheel arches)

Above

A. E. Dean's 1949 Silver Wraith. Another majestic car gliding its way to the Rolls-Royce Enthusiasts meet at Althorp in 1994. This one is a Freestone and Webb Limousine, not only noted for their exterior looks but also for their excellent final detail and very well finished interiors. It has chassis no. WFC 32 and registration no. UMV 80

Above right

Miss D. Nash-Peake's 1949 Silver Wraith. A James Young Saloon in interesting colours for a Rolls-Royce, more often seen on Bentley's. James Young were a Bromley firm founded in 1863 and acquired by J. Barclay in 1937. It has chassis no. WFC 3 and registration No. 566 MWP

Right

1953 Silver Wraith. This Touring Limousine, with coachwork by Freestone and Webb, is extremely impressive. It has chassis no. ALW 39 and registration no. YME 9

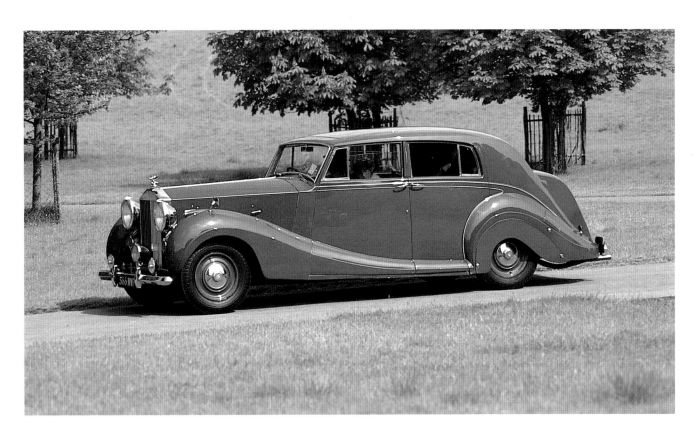

1956 Silver Wraith. This enormous Hooper Limousine has bags of room in the back for tall people. Although a bit heavy to park, once moving they are surprisingly light and easy to manage, with plenty of power on tap if needed. The flags are from Sweden's most southern province. Chassis no. DLW 92 and registration no. PVS 311

Silver Dawn 1949-1954

Apart from the traditional Rolls-Royce method of building a chassis to customer requirements, and then an independent coachbuilder finishing the job (again to customer preference), R-R made a courageous decision after the war – cut production costs by fitting standard bodies of Rolls-Royce design themselves, utilising a pressed steel construction. They also assembled all interior work themselves, including upholstery, finishing and all the paintwork. This new policy ran alongside the old method, and the first models with the new pressed steel bodies now made their appearance, but because of the company's uncertainty on how they would be received by the public, most had the Bentley radiator and were called the Mk. VI.

However, the clamour from America, in particular for a Rolls-Royce, led to the same car being fitted with a Rolls-Royce radiator and automatic gearbox. They were successful as the Silver Dawn, and a new buying public for a complete Rolls-Royce was born, both in America and the UK. They had the same chassis, six-cylinder engine and suspension as the Silver Wraith. These new bodies gave very good accessibility to the engine via a quick release front wing and radiator assembly, whereby the whole lot was removed from the rest of the body. The price of the saloon complete was about £2,500.

R. M. Cannell's 1954 Silver Dawn – a typical Silver Dawn Saloon, about to join in the fun at Althorp in 1994. It has Chassis no. SUJ 24, and Registration no. XWH 1

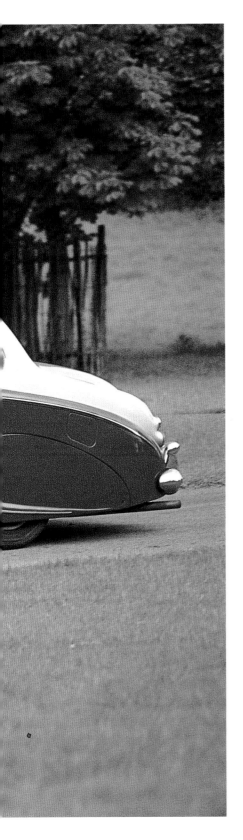

Silver Cloud I 1955-1959

The Silver Cloud, again, used the in-house pressed steel coachwork but was given a new shape, although there were still some made in the old manner of chassis and personally selected coachwork. They were larger with a seventeen foot six inch overall length, compared with the previous sixteen feet. The engine was the same six-cylinder overhead valves and side exhaust as before, but bored out to 92.25mm with the same stroke of 114.3mm, producing 4,887cc and a very reliable block. There was a new cylinder head which had better breathing than before, producing more available power. The chassis was now completely welded, with rivets no longer used, and there were changes in the suspension. It still retained independent front suspension with coil springs and pressed steel wishbones, but the wishbone pivots now had threaded knuckles which were bolted to pressed steel channel section arms. The rear suspension was still semi-elliptic, although now had an anti-roll Z bar.

The dampers were increased in capacity and were still united with the upper pivot. The steering was modified, although still of worm and roller design. The four-speed hydramatic gearbox was kept but given extra clutch plates for prolonged life, bearing in mind the extra weight of the new body. The exhaust was a single system having two silencers and an expansion box in the tail pipe. It ran a tortuous route and required heat-resistant panels underneath the seat pan. Power steering was finally fitted on this model in 1957, and provided ease of steering (of course) but also a surprisingly improved sense of touch. Also in 1957, the engine was fitted with larger carburettors and even larger inlet valves, again improving performance. Chassis price was about £2,550 and the complete car £3,390.

M. Leeman's 1956 Silver Cloud I Sports Saloon. A striking example of the extremely slippery body styles Hooper were now designing. This one also has attractive double headlights. It has chassis no. B 356 CK and registration no. LHZ 451

H. Kay's 1956 Silver Cloud I Saloon. Another Hooper bodied sleek saloon, with a design providing plenty of boot space. It also has fairly unusual front wings with hooded headlights. It has chassis no. SYB 18 and registration no. MSK 684

J. Graham's 1957 Silver Cloud 1. A standard Silver Cloud Sports saloon with the Rolls-Royce bodywork and very pleasant paintwork. It has chassis no. SFE 465 and registration no. WSK 511

R. Allan's 1958 Silver Cloud I. Another Rolls-Royce-designed Sports Saloon on the new chassis, and from any angle a true thoroughbred, oozing quality. It has chassis no. SJF 62 and registration no. 23 AYO